Hamlet: (To himself) "To be, or not to be?" — that is the question.

SHAKESPEARE FOR YOUNG PEOPLE

BOOK 7

HAMLET

FOR
YOUNG PEOPLE

by
William Shakespeare

edited and illustrated by
Diane Davidson

SWAN BOOKS
FAIR OAKS, CALIFORNIA

Published by:

SWAN BOOKS
P.O. Box 2498
Fair Oaks, California 95628

Printed in the United States of America

Library of Congress Cataloging-in-Publication Data

Shakespeare, William, 1564-1616.
    [Hamlet]
    Hamlet for young people / by William Shakespeare ; edited and
illustrated by Diane Davidson.
        p.   cm. -- (Shakespeare for young people ; bk. 7)
    ISBN 0-934048-24-X (pbk.) : $4.95
    1. Denmark--Princes and princess--Juvenile drama. 2. Children's
plays, English.   [1. Plays.]   I. Davidson, Diane. II. Title.
III. Series: Shakespeare, William, 1564-1616. Shakespeare for young
people ; bk. 7.
PR2807.A25   1993b
822.3'3--dc20   93-25861
                                                                 CIP
                                                                  AC

TO THE TEACHER OR PARENT

Young people can grow up loving Shakespeare if they act out his plays. Since Shakespeare wrote for the theater, not for the printed page, he is most exciting on his own ground.

Many people are afraid that the young will not understand Shakespeare's words. To help these actors follow the story, the editor has added two optional announcers, who introduce and explain scenes. However, young people pick up the general meaning with surprising ease, and they enjoy the words without completely understanding them at first. Their ears tell them the phrases often sound like music, and the plays are full of marvelous scenes.

After all, Shakespeare is not called the best of all writers because he is hard. He is the best of all writers because he is enjoyable!

HOW TO BEGIN

At first, students may find the script too difficult to enjoy, so one way to start is for the director to read the play aloud. Between scenes, he can ask, "What do you think is going to happen next?" or "Do you think the characters should do this?" After the students become familiar with the story and words, they can try out for parts by reading different scenes. In the end, the director should pick the actors he thinks are best, emphasizing, "There are no small parts. Everybody helps in a production."

The plays can be presented in several ways.

In the simplest form, the students can read the script aloud, sitting in their seats. This will do well enough, but it is more fun to put on the actual show.

What can a director do to help his actors?

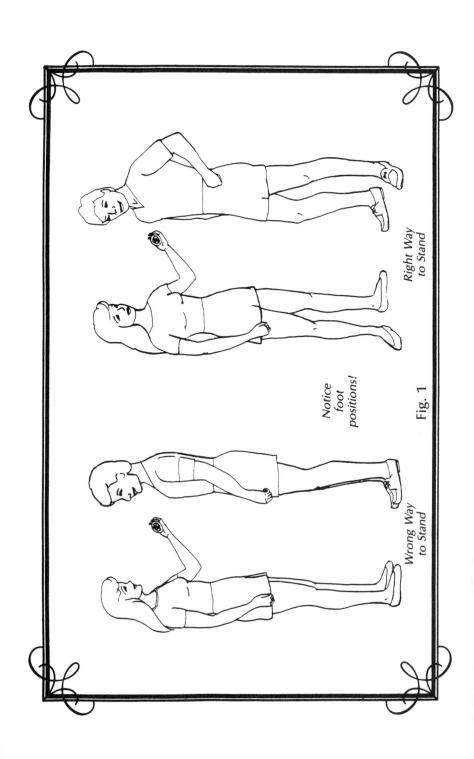

Right Way
to Stand

Notice
foot
positions!

Fig. 1

Wrong Way
to Stand

One main point in directing is to have the actors speak the words loudly and clearly. It helps if they speak a little more slowly than usual. They should not be afraid to pause or to emphasize short phrases. However, they should not try to be "arty" or stilted. Shakespeare wrote very energetic plays.

A second main point in directing is to keep the students facing the audience, even if they are talking to someone else. They should "fake front," so that their bodies face the audience and their heads are only half-way towards the other actors. (Fig. 1)

The cast should be told that when the announcers speak between scenes, servants can continue to change the stage set, and actors can enter, exit, or stand around pretending to talk silently. But if an announcer speaks during a scene, the actors should "freeze" until the announcer has finished his lines. At no time should the actors look at the announcers. (The announcers' parts may be cut out if the director so desires.)

Encouragement and applause inspire the young to do better, and criticism should always be linked with a compliment. Often, letting the students find their own way through the play produces the best results. And telling them, "Mean what you say," or "Be more energetic!" is all they really need.

SCHEDULES AND BUDGET

Forty-five minutes a day—using half the time for group scenes and half the time for individual scenes—is generally enough for students to rehearse. The director should encourage all to learn their lines as soon as possible. An easy way to memorize lines is to tape them and have the student listen to the tape at home each evening, going over it four or five times. Usually actors learn faster by ear than by eye. In all, it takes about six weeks to prepare a good show.

The play seems more complete if it has an audience, even other people from next door. But an afternoon or evening public performance is better yet. The director should announce the show well in advance. A PTA meeting, Open House, a Renaissance Fair, a holiday—all are excellent times to do a play.

To attract a good crowd, the admission should be very small or free. However, a Drama Fund is always useful, so some groups pass a hat, or parents sell cookies and punch. But the best way to raise money for a Drama Fund is to sell advertising in the program. A business-card size ad can sell for $5 to $10, and a larger ad brings in even more. This is money gained well in advance of the show. It can be used for costumes or small 250-500 watt spotlights that can be mounted anywhere. Until there is money in the Drama Fund, the director often becomes an expert at borrowing and improvising. Fortunately, Shakespeare's plays can be produced with almost no scenery or special costumes, and there are no royalties to pay.

SPECIAL NOTES ON THIS PLAY

Hamlet needs only simple staging: two "wings" or screens on each side of the playing area and a couple of screens making an open alcove at the back. If the school has a stage, fine. But good shows can take place at one end of a room. (See Fig. 2)

What can people use as screens? Tall cardboard refrigerator boxes are good. Stage flats, frames of 1″ x 4″ lumber joined by triangles of plywood and covered with muslin sheeting, are excellent if little side flats are hinged to the main one, to provide bracing. A tall ladder can also be a brace, especially for the screen where a curtain must be hung for characters to hide behind.

The alcove at the back is helpful to show special areas by simple effects. A double throne indicates a throne room, or

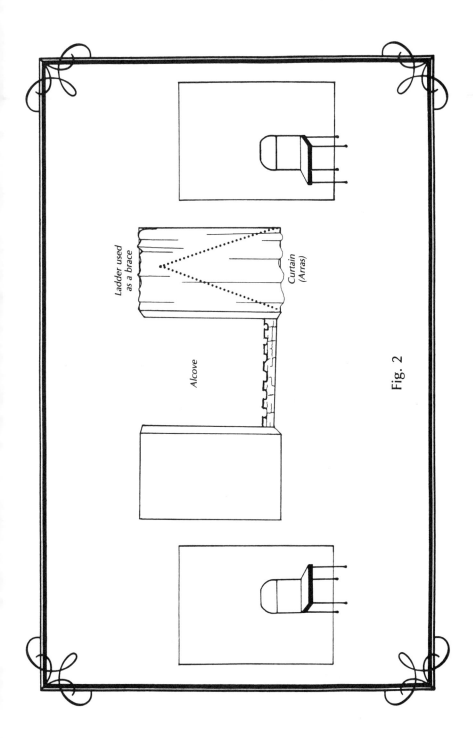

Ladder used as a brace

Curtain (Arras)

Alcove

Fig. 2

a bench covered with drapery becomes a bed. "Ground row" strips of scenery give the effect of a castle tower, seacoast or even a graveyard. (See Figs. 2 and 3.)

On each side of the stage should be chairs where the two announcers sit during the scenes.

Hamlet is usually performed in medieval or Renaissance costumes. Draperies make excellent material, often donated by thrift shops or dry cleaners with unclaimed goods. Older men wear dark full-length robes richly trimmed. Younger men and servants wear tunics or short pants with tights, plus full blouses (ladies' blouses, belted, with sleeves puffed by several elastic bands, do very well). Travelers wear long cloaks. Ladies' dresses have long sleeves and full-length skirts. To show their kinship, Polonius, Laertes and Ophelia should wear the same color clothes or trim. The King, Queen, and Prince Hamlet wear crowns. The Queen and Hamlet wear medallion portraits on chains around their necks. Fortinbras and the Norwegian Captain should look distinctive, wearing red cloaks or elaborate helmets, for example.

A word of warning is necessary: though the actors may have swords, no one is to use them without careful rehearsal, each stroke choreographed and memorized in regular order. Never let the actors improvise, even with imitation swords, as someone may be hurt.

For background music, use something serious with a few exciting parts. The orchestral music of Wagner's *Ring* cycle is excellent, especially "Forest Murmurs" for Ophelia's scenes, "Siegfried's Funeral" and "The End of the Gods (Götterdammerung)."

A LAST BIT OF ADVICE

How will a director know if he has produced Shakespeare "correctly"? He should ask his group if they had fun. If they answer, "Yes," then the show is a success!

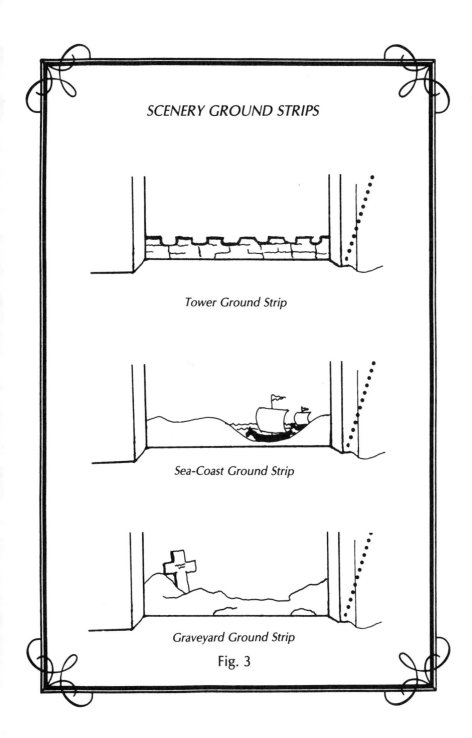

SCENERY GROUND STRIPS

Tower Ground Strip

Sea-Coast Ground Strip

Graveyard Ground Strip

Fig. 3

CHARACTERS

Two Announcers (optional), who have been added

The Royal Family
> Old King Hamlet's Ghost
> Hamlet, the young Prince, a university student
> King Claudius, [**Claw**-dee-us] Old King Hamlet's brother and Prince Hamlet's uncle, a heavy drinker
> Queen Gertrude, Hamlet's widowed mother, now the wife of Claudius, her former brother-in-law

The Chief Minister's Family
> Polonius, [Poh-**loh**-nee-us] the foolish chief minister
> Laertes, [Lay-**air**-teez] his son, a university student
> Ophelia, [O-**fee**-lee-uh] his beautiful daughter

Danish Courtiers and Commoners
> Horatio [Hor-**ay**-shee-oh], Hamlet's good friend
> Rosencrantz and Guildenstern, Hamlet's classmates from Wittenberg University, the King's spies
> Castle Guards: Marcellus, Bernardo, and Francisco
> Osric [**Oz**-rick], a judge of sword-fighting
> First Player in a troupe of traveling actors
> Churchmen: Sexton (a gravedigger) and Priest
> Servants, Other Players, Lords, and Ladies

Strangers in Denmark
> Young Fortinbras [**For**-tin-brahs], Prince of Norway
> Norwegian Captain
> A Pirate

ACT I

(A ground strip shows that the scene is the castle tower. The two announcers enter, bow and take their places on each side of the stage area.)

Announcer 1: (To the audience) Welcome, everyone, to a production of Shakespeare's *Hamlet* given by the _____ class.

Announcer 2: This is not the complete play but a very short edition for young people, using the original words.

Announcer 1: We two announcers have been added to the play to help explain any hard parts.

Announcer 2: You will notice some long words, because in Shakespeare's time, people liked to play with big words as a sort of game with sounds.

Announcer 1: This story is about Hamlet, a Danish prince who is called "The Melancholy Dane."

Announcer 2: "Melancholy" means sad or depressed, and Prince Hamlet has much to be depressed about. For one thing, his father has just died suddenly while Hamlet was away at the university.

Announcer 1: And instead of Hamlet's becoming the new king, his Uncle Claudius was elected to the throne.

Announcer 2: The worst problem was this—right after Hamlet's father died, Hamlet's mother married Claudius, her former brother-in-law.

Announcer 1: In those days, people thought that marrying a brother-in-law was as bad as marrying a
real brother. So Hamlet's mother caused a great
scandal. Hamlet feels trapped in misery.

Announcer 2: But Hamlet's life changes when, late
at night on the castle tower, a ghost begins to walk.
It is Hamlet's father, come back from the dead!

*(One guard, Francisco, appears behind the tower
strip. A second guard, Bernardo, enters on the
main stage, and Francisco whirls, frightened, his
spear ready to strike. He peers into the dark.)*

Bernardo: (Nervously) Who's there?

Francisco: Bernardo? *(With relief, they recognize each
other and relax a little.)*

Bernardo: Tis now struck twelve. Get thee to bed,
Francisco. *(He takes the spear from Francisco, who
steps over the ground strip onto the main stage.)*

Francisco: For this relief much thanks! Tis bitter
cold, and I am sick at heart. *(He shivers.)*

Bernardo: If you do meet Horatio and Marcellus, bid
them make haste. *(He grips the spear, alert.)*

Francisco: I think I hear them. *(Horatio and Marcellus enter.)* Give you good night! *(He leaves.)*

Bernardo: Welcome, Horatio! Welcome, good Marcellus! *(They shake hands. Marcellus is fearful but
Horatio is not.)*

Horatio: (Calmly looking around) What, has this
"Thing" appeared again tonight?

Marcellus: (To Bernardo) Horatio says tis but our "fantasy," this dreaded sight twice seen of us. *(A church clock strikes one. Marcellus points offstage.)* Peace! Look where "It" comes again!

Bernardo: In the same figure like the King that's dead!

(Behind the tower strip comes the Ghost of Old King Hamlet, wearing armor, moving slowly.)

Marcellus: (His voice quavering) Speak to it, Horatio!

Horatio: (Suddenly fearful, he goes towards it.) By Heaven, I charge thee, speak! *(The Ghost exits.)*

Marcellus: Tis gone, and will not answer!

Bernardo: How now, Horatio! You tremble and look pale. Is not this something more than "fantasy"?

Horatio: (Amazed) I might not this believe, without mine own eyes! *(The Ghost returns.)* Lo, where it comes again! Stay, Illusion! *(The Ghost turns towards him.)* If thou hast any voice, speak to me! *(The Ghost opens its mouth to speak when a rooster crows. Then the Ghost shudders and glides away.)*

Bernardo: It was about to speak when the cock crew!

Horatio: And then it started like a guilty thing! *(He points to the sky, where the red-cloaked dawn appears.)* But, look, the morn in russet mantle clad walks o'er the dew of yon high eastern hill. *(He makes a suggestion.)* By my advice, let us impart what we have seen tonight unto Young Hamlet. For, upon my life, this Spirit—dumb to us—will speak to **him**! *(The others nod agreement.)*

Marcellus: Let's do it, I pray! *(They leave together.)*

(Servants remove the tower strip and put two thrones in the alcove. King Claudius and Queen Gertrude enter and sit on the thrones. Polonius, Laertes and other courtiers stand on each side. All raise glasses in a toast. Hamlet, dressed in black, stands to one side, looking at the floor sadly.)

Announcer 1: Meanwhile, King Claudius and Queen Gertrude are celebrating their new marriage.

Announcer 2: Still, King Claudius tries to sound a little sad about his brother's death.

King: Though of Hamlet, our dear brother's death, the memory be green, yet our sometime-sister, now our Queen, have we taken to wife! *(All cheer and drink. Hamlet frowns. The King smiles.)* For all—our thanks! *(As the Queen takes the King's glass, Polonius hands him a letter.)*

Announcer 1: Now the new King faces a national problem: an invasion by Prince Fortinbras of Norway, whose father lost some land to Old King Hamlet.

King: Now follows that you know—Young Fortinbras. He hath not failed to pester us with the surrender of those lands lost by his father to our most valiant brother. *(He tears up the letter.)* So much for him! *(The court cheers. Polonius hands the King another letter and a feather pen.)*

Announcer 2: King Claudius asks the King of Norway to stop the warlike Prince.

King: We have here writ to Norway, uncle of Young Fortinbras, to suppress his further gait. *(He signs the second letter and hands it to Polonius, who bows and brings Laertes forward a little.)*

Announcer 1: The King's chief councillor is Polonius, whose son Laertes goes to a university in France.

King: (To Laertes.) And now, Laertes, what's the news with you? *(Laertes kneels.)* What wouldst thou have, Laertes? *(The King takes his glass and drinks.)*

Laertes: My lord, your leave to return to France!

King: Have you your father's leave? *(He looks at the gray-bearded minister.)* What says Polonius?

Polonius: (Smiling) He hath, my lord. I do beseech you give him leave to go!

King: (Smiling also) Take thy fair hour, Laertes. *(Laertes and Polonius bow and leave happily. The King now frowns at mournful Hamlet.)* But now, my cousin Hamlet and my son—how is it that the clouds still hang on you?

Hamlet: (Looking at the King's glittering crown.) Not so, my lord. I am too much "in the sun."

Announcer 2: The King and Queen want Hamlet to stop looking so miserable about his dead father.

Queen: Good Hamlet, cast thy nighted color off! Thou knowest tis common—all that lives must die.

Hamlet: (Quietly) Ay, madam, it is common.

Queen: If it be, why seems it so particular with thee?

Hamlet: "Seems," madam? Nay, it **is**! *(He points at his black cloak.)* Tis not alone my inky cloak, good mother, nor customary suits of solemn black—these indeed "seem." *(He grips at his aching heart.)* But I have that **within** which passes show!

King: (Sharply) Hamlet, you must know your father lost a father. That father lost, lost his. Tis unmanly grief! *(In a kinder voice)* Think of **us** as a father. *(Hamlet turns away, disgusted.)* For your going back to school in Wittenberg, we beseech you to remain here! *(He drinks.)*

Queen: (Sweetly to her son) I pray thee, stay with us!

Hamlet: (To the Queen with real affection.) I shall, in all my best, obey **you**, madam.

King: (Smiling) Why, tis a loving and a fair reply. *(He holds out his hand to the Queen, who smiles at him.)* Come away! *(They leave with the courtiers.)*

Announcer 1: But Hamlet wishes he could melt away or that God had not forbidden suicide.

Hamlet: (To himself, as he sits on the throne.) O that this too, too-solid flesh would melt, thaw, and resolve itself into a dew! Or that the Everlasting had not fixed his canon 'gainst self-slaughter!

Announcer 2: He thinks of his fine dead father, whose picture he always wears around his neck.

Hamlet: (Looking at the picture.) That it should come to this . . . but two months dead, . . . nay, not so much, not two. So excellent a King! *(He sighs.)* Heaven and earth, must I remember?

Announcer 1: He thinks of his weak mother.

Hamlet: And yet within a month—Frailty, thy name is woman!—within a month, she ... **married!** But break, my heart, for I must hold my tongue!

Announcer 2: Now Hamlet's friends come to tell him of the Ghost. *(Horatio, Marcellus and Bernardo enter.)*

Horatio: (Bowing) Hail to your lordship!

Hamlet: (Absent-mindedly) I am glad to see you well. *(Then he sees his best friend Horatio and runs to hug him eagerly.)* Horatio, or I do forget myself! *(To the others, shaking hands.)* I am very glad to see you. *(To Horatio)* My good friend, what make you from Wittenberg?

Horatio: My lord, I came to see your father's funeral.

Hamlet: Do not mock me, fellow-student. *(Bitterly)* I think it was to see my mother's wedding.

Horatio: Indeed, my lord, it followed hard upon.

Announcer 1: Hamlet pretends the marriage saved money, using leftover food from the funeral.

Hamlet: Thrift, thrift, Horatio. The funeral-baked meats did coldly furnish forth the marriage tables. *(He stares off into the distance dreamily.)* My father ... methinks I see my father ....

Horatio: (Looking about for the Ghost.) Where, my lord?

Hamlet: (Sadly) In my mind's eye, Horatio. *(Remembering)* He was a man, take him for all in all! I shall not look upon his like again. *(He turns away.)*

Horatio: (Carefully breaking the news.) My lord, I think I saw him yesternight.

Hamlet: Saw? Who?

Horatio: My lord, . . . the King, your father! *(He and the guards nod together.)*

Hamlet: (Shocked) The King my father? For God's love, let me hear!

Horatio: Two nights together had these gentlemen, Marcellus and Bernardo, on their watch, in the dead waste and middle of the night, been thus encountered: a figure like your father, armed, appears before them. Thrice he walked! And I with them the third night kept the watch. I **knew** your father! *(He shows his hands.)* These hands are not more like!

Hamlet: (Amazed) Did you not speak to it?

Horatio: My lord, I did. But answer made it none.

Hamlet: Tis very strange! *(Excited)* Hold you the watch tonight?

All: We do, my lord!

Hamlet: (Checking the facts) Armed, say you?

All: Armed, my lord.

Hamlet: I will watch tonight. Perchance 'twill walk again! *(He puts his finger to his lips.)* I pray you all, your silence still. Upon the platform twixt eleven and twelve, I'll visit you. *(He shakes their hands.)* Farewell! *(They bow and leave. Restlessly he speaks to himself.)* My father's spirit . . . in arms! All is not well. Would the night were come! Till then, sit still, my soul . . . . *(He too leaves.)*

(The servants take off the thrones. Laertes and Ophelia enter with a servant carrying bundles.)

Announcer 2: Laertes says farewell to his pretty sister, Ophelia.

Laertes: (Waving the servant to leave.) My necessaries are embarked. *(He takes Ophelia's hand.)* And, Sister, do not sleep but let me hear from you!

Ophelia: (Sweetly) Do you doubt that?

Announcer 1: He warns her not to take Hamlet's love seriously. The Prince is too high-born for her.

Laertes: For Hamlet and the "trifling of his favor," hold it a fashion—sweet, not lasting—no more.

Ophelia: (Disappointed) No more but so?

Laertes: Perhaps he loves you now, but his will is not his own. He himself is subject to his birth.

Ophelia: (Obediently) I shall the effect of this good lesson keep as watchman to my heart! *(He gives her a hug as their father, Polonius, enters.)*

Polonius: (Hurrying him off) Laertes! Abroad, abroad, for shame! The wind sits in the shoulder of your sail. *(Polonius puts his hand on his son's head.)* There . . . My blessing with thee! *(Laertes smiles.)*

Announcer 2: Polonius then gives his son some good advice: to talk little, keep friends, not to fight, to wear good clothes but not fancy ones, not to borrow or lend, and to be truthful.

Polonius: (Putting his arm about his son's shoulder.) And these few precepts in thy memory see thou character: Give thy thoughts no tongue. The friends thou hast, grapple them to thy soul with hoops of steel. Beware of entrance to a quarrel. Give every man thine ear, but few thy voice. *(He straightens Laertes' jacket.)* Costly thy habit as thy purse can buy. Rich, not gaudy, for the apparel oft proclaims the man. Neither a borrower nor a lender be. *(A final serious thought)* This above all—to thine own self be true, and it must follow, as the night the day, thou canst not then be false to any man. *(With a smile and a hug.)* Farewell!

Laertes: I take my leave, my lord. *(To his sister)* Farewell, Ophelia, and remember well what I have said to you! *(With a quick kiss, he leaves.)*

Polonius: What is it, Ophelia, he hath said to you?

Ophelia: (Shyly) Something touching the Lord Hamlet.

Polonius: (Worried) What is between you?

Ophelia: (Blushing) My lord, he hath importuned me with love in honorable fashion!

Polonius: (Sharply) Ophelia, do not believe his vows!

Announcer 1: The old courtier forbids Ophelia to see the Prince again. Such a romance must stop!

Polonius: (Very sternly) This is for all—I would not from this time forth have you give words or talk with the Lord Hamlet. Look to it, I charge you!

Ophelia: (Heartbroken) I shall obey. *(They exit.)*

(Servants put on the tower ground strip. Hamlet, Horatio, and Marcellus enter wearing cloaks.)

Announcer 2: Late at night, Hamlet and his friends go to the castle tower to speak to the Ghost.

Hamlet: (Shivering) It is very cold. What hour now?

Horatio: I think it lacks of twelve. *(The Ghost enters behind the tower strip.)* Look, my lord!

Hamlet: (Making the Sign of the Cross in fear.) Angels and ministers of grace defend us! *(To the Ghost)* I'll call thee Hamlet . . . King . . . Father . . . Royal Dane! O answer me! *(The Ghost waves for Hamlet to come.)*

Horatio: It beckons you to go away with it!

Hamlet: It will not speak! *(His friends hold him back but he tears himself away, calling to the Ghost.)* Go on! I'll follow thee! *(The Ghost exits as Hamlet leaps the low wall and follows cautiously.)*

Marcellus: (Worried) Something is rotten in the state of Denmark. Let's follow him! *(Slowly and fearfully, he and Horatio go after their Prince.)*

Ghost: I am thy father's spirit, doomed for a certain term to walk the night.

(The Ghost re-enters with Hamlet close behind.)

Hamlet: (Stopping) Speak! I'll go no further.

Ghost: (Raising his hand for attention.) Mark me!

Hamlet: I am bound to hear! *(He kneels to listen.)*

Announcer 1: The Ghost tells Hamlet he was murdered.

Ghost: I am thy father's spirit, doomed for a certain term to walk the night, and for the day confined to fast in fires. *(Pleading)* If thou didst ever thy dear father love . . . revenge his foul and most unnatural murder!

Hamlet: (Horrified) Murder?

Ghost: Murder most foul. Now, Hamlet, hear! Tis given out that, sleeping in my orchard, a serpent stung me. But know, thou noble youth, the "serpent" that did sting thy father's life now wears his crown!

Hamlet: O my prophetic soul . . . my uncle!

Announcer 2: The Ghost tells how Hamlet's Uncle Claudius poured poison in his ear.

Ghost: Ay, that beast! *(Angrily)* Sleeping within my orchard, upon my hour thy uncle stole with juice of cursed hebenon in a vial, and in the porches of mine ears did pour the leperous distilment. Thus was I, sleeping, by a brother's hand cut off. O horrible, O horrible, most horrible! *(A rooster crows. The Ghost listens and leaves slowly.)* Adieu, adieu, adieu! Remember me! *(He is gone.)*

Hamlet: Remember thee? *(A promise)* Yes, by Heaven!

Horatio: (Calling) My lord, my lord! *(He and Marcellus enter, greeting Hamlet with relief.)*

Marcellus: How is it, my noble lord?

Hamlet: (Sharply) Never make known what you have seen tonight! *(He glances back where the Ghost left.)*

Both: My lord, we will not!

Hamlet: Nay, but swear it. Upon my sword! *(He reverses his sword so it forms a Cross and holds it out.)*

Ghost's Voice: (Offstage) Swear! *(The men are fearful, but they put their hands on the sword to swear.)*

Horatio: This is wondrous strange!

Hamlet: (Mysteriously) There are more things in Heaven and earth, Horatio, than are dreamt of in your philosophy. *(He puts his sword in his belt.)* So, gentlemen, let us go in together. *(He gestures to his mouth.)* And still your fingers on your lips, I pray. *(Feeling his world has grown crooked, he stops, uneasy.)* The time is "out of joint." O cursèd spite, that ever **I** was born to set it right! *(His friends lead him off, worried.)*

ACT II

(Servants remove the tower strip and put the thrones in the alcove. Polonius enters reading a book.)

Announcer 1: Hamlet cannot decide what to do exactly. He needs more proof of his father's murder.

Announcer 2: To conceal his suspicions, he pretends to be insane. He begins with frightening Ophelia. *(Ophelia runs in, terrified, to her father.)*

Polonius: (Opening his arms to protect her.) How now, Ophelia. What's the matter?

Ophelia: (Pointing to her room.) As I was sewing in my closet, Lord Hamlet—with his doublet all unbraced, no hat upon his head, his stockings down to his ankle, pale as his shirt—he comes before me!

Polonius: Mad for thy love?

Ophelia: Truly I do fear it! He took me by the wrist and held me hard. Then goes he to the length of all his arm. At last, thrice his head waving up and down, he raised a sigh. That done, he lets me go. And with his head over his shoulder turned, he seemed to find his way without his eyes, for out-of-doors he went without their help!

Polonius: Have you given him any hard words of late?

Announcer 1: Ophelia has broken off their romance.

Ophelia: As you did command, I did repel his letters and denied his access to me. *(She hands him a letter, which he glances at.)*

Polonius: (Convinced) That hath made him mad! Come, go we to the King! *(They leave hurriedly.)*

Announcer 2: To find out why Hamlet has suddenly gone mad, the King invites two of the prince's classmates to Elsinore Castle to act as spies.

(The King, Queen, Rosencrantz and Guildenstern enter. The King carries his usual wine goblet.)

King: (To the young men) Welcome, dear Rosencrantz and Guildenstern! The need we have to use you did provoke our hasty sending. Something have you heard of Hamlet's "transformation." I entreat you both, instantly visit my too-much changed son to gather whether aught afflicts him thus!

Guildenstern: We both obey. *(They bow and leave as Polonius enters with the letter. The King drinks.)*

Polonius: (With a hasty bow) My lord, I do think that I have found the very cause of Hamlet's lunacy!

King: O speak of that. That do I long to hear!

Polonius: (With foolish self-importance) Your noble son is mad! "Mad" call I it, for to define true madness, what is it but to be nothing else but . . . mad? But let that go . . . . That he is mad, tis true. Tis true, tis pity. And pity tis, tis true! *(He laughs, then coughs, turning serious.)* I have a daughter who hath given me this. *(He reads from the letter.)*

> "Doubt thou the stars are fire,
> Doubt that the sun doth move,

Doubt truth to be a liar
But never doubt I love!
"O dear Ophelia, I love thee best, believe it!
Hamlet"

King: (To the Queen) Do you think tis this?

Queen: (Nodding) It may be, very like.

Announcer 1: The King wants to test the idea that Hamlet is crazy because of love.

King: How may we try it further?

Polonius: You know sometimes he walks here in the lobby? At such a time, I'll loose my daughter to him. *(He pulls out the curtain a little.)* Be you and I behind an arras then!

King: (Very interested) We will try it! *(He drinks.)*

(Enter Hamlet, his clothes buttoned wrong, his hair mussed, and his stockings sagging. He is reading.)

Polonius: (Hurrying them off.) Away, I do beseech you! *(After they leave, he speaks to the Prince to observe his madness.)* What do you read, my lord?

Hamlet: Words, words, words . . . . *(Pointing to the book)* The rogue says here that old men have grey beards, that their faces are wrinkled. *(Inspecting Polonius)* For yourself, sir, shall grow old as I am, if like a crab you could go backward. *(He laughs wildly.)*

Polonius: (To himself) Though this be madness, yet there is method in it! *(He tries more conversation.)* Will you walk out of the air, my lord?

Hamlet: (Sadly) Into my grave?

Polonius: Indeed, that **is** out of the air! *(Bowing)* My lord, I will most humbly take my leave of you.

Hamlet: (Sorrowfully) You cannot, sir, take from me anything that I will more willingly part withal—except my life, except my life, except my life! *(He watches Polonius go.)* These tedious old fools!

Announcer 2: Now Rosencrantz and Guildenstern come, as the King's spies, to see why Hamlet is mad.

Guildenstern: (Entering with Rosencrantz) My lord!

Hamlet: (Happy to see them) My excellent good friends! How dost thou, Guildenstern? Ah, Rosencrantz! *(He hugs them both, but they smile uneasily. He gives them a sharp glance, and his smile fades.)* What have you, my good friends, deserved at the hands of Fortune, that she sends you to prison hither?

Guildenstern: (With a false smile) Prison, my lord?

Hamlet: (Bitterly) Denmark's a prison!

Rosencrantz: We think not so, my lord.

Hamlet: Why then, tis none to you. *(Thoughtfully)* For there is nothing either good or bad, but thinking makes it so . . . . *(Trying to be cheerful)* But in the way of friendship, what make you at Elsinore?

Rosencrantz: (Awkwardly) To visit you, my lord.

Hamlet: I thank you! And sure, dear friends, were

you not sent for? Is it a free visitation? *(The two men exchange glances.)* Come, come . . . nay, speak!

Guildenstern: (Uneasily) What should we say, my lord?

Hamlet: (Realizing they are spies.) Why, I know the good King and Queen have sent for you.

Guildenstern: (Confessing) My lord, we **were** sent for!

Announcer 1: Hamlet explains how he has been depressed lately. All the world seems a desert cliff, and the sky is an evil fog.

Hamlet: I will tell you why. I have of late—but wherefore I know not—lost all my mirth, forgone all custom of exercises. And, indeed, it goes so heavily with my disposition, that this goodly frame, the earth, seems to me a sterile promontory. *(He points upward.)* This most excellent canopy, the air—look you! This brave o'erhanging firmament, this majestical roof fretted with golden fire—why, it appears no other thing to me than a foul and pestilent congregation of vapors!

Announcer 2: Even mankind, so marvelous, gives no joy.

Hamlet: (He looks at his hand in wonder.) What a piece of work is man! How noble in reason! In action, how like an angel! In apprehension, how like a god! The beauty of the world, the paragon of animals! *(He drops his hand sadly.)* And yet, man delights not me. *(His schoolmates laugh. Hamlet frowns.)* . . . No, nor woman neither, though by your smiling you seem to say so.

Rosencrantz: (Hastily) There was no such stuff in my thoughts! To think, my lord—if you delight not in man, what entertainment the players shall receive from you! *(He points offstage.)*

Hamlet: What players are they? *(A trumpet call rings out. Hamlet smiles at the sound, and hurries the spies off with a silly joke.)* Gentlemen, welcome! But my uncle-father and aunt-mother are deceived!

Guildenstern: (Eagerly) In what, my dear lord?

Hamlet: (With scorn) I am but mad north-north-west! *(He taps his head wisely.)* When the wind is southerly, I know a hawk from a handsaw!

(He waves the spies away as Polonius enters with the traveling actors, who bow, some turning cartwheels or playing flutes and drums.)

Polonius: (Announcing) The actors are come hither, my lord! The best actors in the world, either for tragedy, comedy, history, pastoral, pastoral-comical, historical-pastoral, tragical-historical, tragical-comical-historical-pastoral, scene individable or poem unlimited! These are the only men! *(Out of breath but pleased, he smiles foolishly.)*

Hamlet: (To the actors, shaking their hands.) You are welcome, masters, welcome all! *(To the leader, fondly.)* Come, a passionate speech!

First Player: (Smiling) What speech, my good lord?

Hamlet: I heard thee once . . . Twas Aeneas' [A-**nee**-us] tale to Dido [**Die**-doh], where he speaks of Priam's [**Pry**-am's] slaughter. *(He smiles, waiting.)*

Announcer 1: The actor tells of the Trojan War, where Queen Hecuba [**Heck**-u-bah] sees her husband Priam cut to pieces.

First Player: (Standing with dignity to recite.)
The hellish Pyrrhus [**Peer**-us] old grandsire
Priam seeks.
Anon he finds him! Unequal matched,
Pyrrhus at Priam drives, in rage strikes wide,
But the unnerved father falls.
But who—O, who had seen the mobled Queen
Run barefoot up and down
When she saw Pyrrhus make malicious sport
In mincing with his sword her husband's
limbs . . . .
(His voice falters and he stops, weeping.)

Polonius: Look where he has not turned his color and has tears in his eyes!

Hamlet: (Hurrying to put his arm about the Player's shoulders in sympathy.) Tis well. *(To Polonius)* Good my lord, will you see the players well bestowed? Take them in. *(All leave but the First Player, whose arm Hamlet takes.)* We'll hear a play tomorrow. Can you play "The Murder of Gonzago"?

First Player: (Wiping his tears) Ay, my lord.

Hamlet: (With kindness) We'll have it tomorrow night! *(The First Player bows with gratitude and leaves. Hamlet sinks down on the throne.)* Now I am alone.

Announcer 2: Hamlet hates himself for not weeping over his father, as the actor cried over Queen Hecuba.

Hamlet: *(Striking his fist into his hand in anger.)* O what a rogue and peasant slave am I! Is it not monstrous that this player here—but in a fiction, in a dream of passion—could force his soul so all his visage wanned, tears in his eyes, a broken voice—and all for nothing. For Hecuba! What's Hecuba to him or he to Hecuba, that he should weep for her? *(He sighs and shakes his head.)*

What would he do, had he the motive and the cue for passion that I have? He would drown the stage with tears! *(He clasps his hands to his chest.)* Yet I, a dull and muddy-mettled rascal, can say nothing! *(A new thought occurs.)* Am I a coward?

(He rises and looks at the throne.) Bloody villain! Remorseless, treacherous, lecherous, kindless villain! *(A howl of fury)* O vengeance!

(He tries to think, holding his hands to his head.) About, my brain . . . .

Announcer 1: He plans to prove the King's guilt in front of everyone at the play tomorrow night.

Hamlet: *(With decision)* I'll have these players play something like the murder of my father before mine uncle. I'll observe his looks. For Murder, though it have no tongue, will **speak**! *(Excited)* The play's the thing wherein I'll catch the conscience of the King! *(Desperately hopeful, he runs off.)*

ACT III

(Polonius, the King and Ophelia enter the same scene.)

Announcer 1: Polonius still wants to prove Hamlet's madness is caused by hopeless love for Ophelia.

Polonius: (Pointing) Ophelia, walk you here. *(He hands her a prayerbook.)* Read on this book. I hear him coming! *(To the King)* Let's withdraw, my lord.

(He and the King hide behind the curtain. Ophelia stands far to one side as Hamlet enters, not noticing her. Restless, he sits on the throne and draws his dagger, pointing it towards himself.)

Announcer 2: Uncertain about everything, Hamlet thinks of life and death.

Announcer 1: He wonders—is it better to suffer life's troubles or to commit suicide?

Hamlet: (To himself) "To be, or not to be?"—that is the question. Whether tis nobler in the mind to suffer the slings and arrows of outrageous fortune, or . . . *(He tests the dagger point with his finger.)* . . . to take arms against a sea of troubles and, by opposing, end them? *(He starts to stab himself, shakes his head sadly, and thinks more.)*

Announcer 2: Death looks like sleep, but it may have unknown nightmares.

Hamlet: To die, to sleep . . . to sleep . . . perchance to dream! *(He frowns.)* Ay, there's the rub! For in that "sleep of death," what **dreams** may come must give us pause!

Announcer 1: So people suffer the miseries of life, rather than face the unknown world of death.

Hamlet: For who would bear the whips and scorns of time, the pangs of despised love, the law's delay, to grunt and sweat under a weary life, but that the dread of "something" after death puzzles the will, and makes us rather bear those ills we have, than fly to others that we know not of. Thus conscience does make cowards of us all . . . . *(He sees Ophelia.)* Soft you now—the fair Ophelia! *(He goes to her.)*

Ophelia: *(Embarrassed)* Good my lord, how does your honor for this many a day? *(She looks at the arras curtain where her father and the King are hiding.)*

Hamlet: I humbly thank you, well . . . well . . . well! *(He too looks at the arras, which is bulging.)*

Ophelia: *(Taking love gifts from her pocket.)* My lord, I have remembrances of yours that I have longed to re-deliver. I pray you, now receive them. *(She hands them to him, but he pushes them away.)*

Hamlet: *(Tenderly)* I did love you once . . . .

Ophelia: Indeed, my lord, you made me believe so!

Hamlet: *(Looking at the curtain)* You should not have believed me. *(Harshly)* I loved you not!

Announcer 2: Hamlet tells Ophelia to become a nun.

Hamlet: Believe none of us! Go thy ways to a nunnery! *(Looking at the arras)* Where's your father?

Ophelia: *(Obviously lying)* At home, my lord.

Hamlet: *(Disgusted)* Get thee to a nunnery. Go! Farewell! It hath made me mad! I say we will have no more marriages! To a nunnery, go! *(He rushes off, and Ophelia sinks to the ground in tears.)*

Announcer 1: Ophelia thinks her perfect Prince is mad.

Ophelia: *(Looking after Hamlet)* O, what a noble mind is here o'erthrown! The glass of fashion and the mould of form—quite, quite down. O woe is me—to have seen what I have seen, see what I see!

Announcer 2: The King does not think Hamlet is love-sick or mad. He decides to send him to England.

King: *(Coming from behind the arras with Polonius.)* Love? His affections do not that way tend. Nor what he spake was not like madness. *(With decision)* He shall with speed to England! *(To Polonius)* What think you on it?

Polonius: It shall do well. *(To his daughter, gently)* How now, Ophelia? *(She cries.)* We heard it all. *(They leave, helping the weeping Ophelia.)*

Announcer 1: Meanwhile Hamlet tells the Players how to speak and act naturally in the play that evening. *(Hamlet and Players enter.)*

Hamlet: Speak the speech, I pray you, as I pronounced it to you—trippingly on the tongue. *(He waves his hand stiffly.)* Nor do not saw the air too much with your hand thus, but use all gently. Be not too tame neither. Suit the action to the word, the word to the action. "Hold the mirror up to nature."

(The Players smile and bow. They set a draped bench to one side of the stage, where they will act their play. There they wait. Horatio enters.)

Announcer 2: Hamlet hopes to prove the King guilty now.

Hamlet: (Privately to Horatio.) There is a play tonight before the King. One scene of it comes near the circumstance of my father's death. When thou seest that act afoot, **observe my uncle!**

Horatio: (Nodding seriously) Well, my lord!

(To music, enter Polonius, King, Queen, Ophelia, Rosencrantz, Guildenstern and others. They assemble around the throne.)

(The actors bow. All applaud. The action starts. In pantomime, the Player King and Player Queen kiss. The Player King lies on the bench and goes to sleep. The Player Queen leaves. The Poisoner enters, slowly pours poison into the Player King's ear, and leaves. The Player King gasps and dies. The Player Queen enters and tries to wake the Player King. She silently shrieks. The Poisoner enters and gives her a flower. She refuses it. He plays a flute to woo her. She flutters.)

Hamlet: (To his mother) Madam, how like you this play?

Queen: (Thinking the Player Queen over-acts.) The lady doth protest too much, methinks. *(She frowns.)*

(The Player Queen finally takes the flower, and she and the Poisoner hold hands lovingly.)

King: (In a harsh voice) What do you call the play?

Hamlet: (Excited) "The Mouse-Trap." This play is the image of a murder done in Vienna. *(Pointing)* He poisons him in the garden! The story is written in choice Italian! You shall see anon how the murderer gets the love of Gonzago's wife! *(The King stands, full of guilt.)*

Ophelia: The King rises!

Polonius: (Stopping the actors) Give o'er the play!

King: (Shouting) Give me some light! Away! *(He runs off calling, "Light, light!" The others follow him, except for Hamlet and Horatio.)*

Hamlet: (With joy) O good Horatio, I'll take the Ghost's word for a thousand pound! . . . Did'st **perceive?**

Horatio: (Agreeing eagerly) Very well, my lord!

Hamlet: Upon the talk of the poisoning? *(Horatio nods.)*

Announcer 1: But now the King's spies try even harder to find out why Hamlet is mad.

Guildenstern: (Entering with Rosencrantz, he bows to Hamlet.) Good my lord, the Queen, your mother, desires to speak with you. *(With a wink at his partner, he adds slyly.)* Good my lord, what is your cause of . . . *(He taps his head)* . . . distemper?

Hamlet: (Picking up the wooden flute from the Players' stage.) Oh. *(He hands it to Guildenstern.)* Will you play upon this pipe?

Guildenstern: My lord, I cannot.

Hamlet: Give it breath with your mouth. *(Showing him the holes)* Look you, these are the "stops."

Guildenstern: (Protesting) I have not the skill!

Hamlet: (With anger) Why, look you now, you would play upon **me**. You would seem to know **my** stops. You would pluck out the heart of **my** mystery. *(Giving the flute to Guildenstern.)* You cannot play upon **me**! *(Horatio takes the two spies offstage roughly.)*

Hamlet: (Looking about at the dark.) Tis now the very witching time of night . . . Now to my mother. I will speak daggers to her but use none! *(He exits.)*

(Servants remove the thrones and move the bench to the alcove. The King comes in and kneels to pray, center stage. Hamlet enters behind him but stops.)

Announcer 2: Finally Hamlet can kill the King!

King: (To himself) O my offense is rank. It smells to Heaven—a brother's murder! *(Looking up)* Help, angels! *(With hope)* All may be well! *(He prays.)*

Hamlet: (Drawing his sword) Now might I do it pat! *(He starts to stab the King but hesitates.)* And so he goes to Heaven? *(He sheathes his sword.)* No! When he is drunk or in his rage, **then** trip him, that his soul may be as black as Hell whereto it goes! *(He looks offstage.)* My mother stays. *(He exits.)*

King: (Sadly rising) My words fly up. My thoughts remain below. Words without thoughts never to Heaven go. *(He exits slowly, full of guilt.)*

(Queen Gertrude and Polonius enter. She sits on the bench as he tells her to scold her son.)

Polonius: (Pointing offstage) Look you, lay home to him! Pray you, be round with him!

Queen: Fear me not! Withdraw. I hear him coming. *(Polonius hides behind the arras-curtain. Hamlet enters sternly. His mother is equally stern.)*

Announcer 1: Hamlet wants his mother to see the scandal of her marriage to Claudius.

Hamlet: (Harshly) Now, Mother, what's the matter?

Queen: Hamlet, thou hast thy father much offended!

Hamlet: Mother, you have **my** father much offended!

Queen: Why, how now, Hamlet, have you forgot me?

Hamlet: No, you are your husband's brother's wife, and—would it were not so!—you are my mother!

Queen: (Rising angrily) Nay, then I'll set those to you that can speak!

Hamlet: (Pushing her back down with equal anger.) Come, come, and sit you down. You shall not budge!

Queen: (Frightened) What wilt thou do? Thou wilt not murder me? *(Calling)* Help, ho!

Polonius: (Behind the curtain) What ho! Help!

Hamlet: (Drawing his sword) How now, a rat? *(He lunges at the curtain.)* Dead for a ducat, dead! *(Polonius slumps to the floor.)* Is it the King?

Queen: (Rising) O, what a bloody deed is this!

Hamlet: *(Accusingly)* Almost as bad, good Mother, as kill a King and marry with his brother!

Queen: *(Horrified)* As kill a King?

Hamlet: Ay, lady. *(He lifts up the curtain and sees Polonius dead. He speaks to the old man.)* Thou wretched, rash, intruding fool, farewell. *(The Queen wrings her hands in sorrow.)* Leave wringing of your hands. Peace, sit you down, and let me wring your heart.

Queen: *(Stupidly)* What have I done?

Hamlet: *(Comparing the picture around his neck to the one around hers.)* Look upon this picture, and on this: two brothers. *(Showing his picture)* See what a grace was on this brow! This **was** your husband! *(Showing her the picture of Claudius.)* Look you now what follows. Here **is** your husband, like a mildewed ear, blasting his wholesome brother. Have you eyes? *(She weeps.)* O Shame!

Queen: No more, sweet Hamlet!

Hamlet: A murderer and a villain! *(Dead King Hamlet's Ghost appears. Astonished, Hamlet goes to it slowly and kneels.)* What would your gracious figure?

Queen: *(Horrified, as she sees nothing.)* He's mad!

Ghost: *(To Hamlet, reminding him to take revenge.)* Do not forget! *(Pointing to the Queen.)* But look, amazement on thy mother sits. Speak to her, Hamlet!

Hamlet: *(Still looking at the Ghost.)* How is it with you, lady?

Queen: Whereon do you look? To whom do you speak this?

Hamlet: Do you see nothing there? *(He rises.)*

Queen: Nothing at all, yet all that is, I see!

Hamlet: *(Pointing to the Ghost, who drifts away.)* Why, look you there! My father in his habit as he lived. Look where he goes! *(Pleading)* Mother, for love of grace, confess yourself to Heaven, repent!

Queen: O Hamlet, thou hast cleft my heart in twain!

Hamlet: *(Going to her)* O, throw away the worser part of it. Assume a virtue if you have it not! *(Gently)* Good night. *(He turns to Polonius.)* For this same lord, I do repent. *(To her)* So again, good night. I must be cruel only to be kind. *(He strokes her hair. She weeps.)* I must to England, you know that.

Queen: *(Sobbing, bewildered)* Alack, I had forgot!

Hamlet: There's letters sealed, and my two school-fellows bear the mandate. *(He starts to drag Polonius offstage.)* Come, sir. *(To her)* Good night, Mother! *(He leaves with the body, and Queen Gertrude rushes off hysterically to find help.)*

ACT IV

(Servants remove the bench and put the thrones in the alcove. The King enters with Rosencrantz, Guildenstern and others. The Queen rushes in, crying.)

King: What, Gertrude? How does Hamlet?

Queen: Mad as the sea and wind! *(She points behind her.)* In his lawless fit, behind the arras hearing something stir, whips out his rapier, cries, "A rat, a rat!" and kills the good old man!

King: Alas, where is he gone?

Queen: To draw apart the body he hath killed. *(She shudders as her son enters alone.)*

King: (Sternly) Now, Hamlet, where is Polonius?

Hamlet: (Pointing to the sky) In Heaven. Send thither to see. If your messenger find him not there . . . *(He points downwards with a sneer.)* . . . seek him in the other place yourself!

King: (With decision) Hamlet, prepare thyself. Everything is bent for England!

Hamlet: For England? *(The King nods.)* Good. Farewell, dear Mother. *(He bows to the King.)*

King: (Puzzled) Thy loving **Father**, Hamlet.

Hamlet: Father and mother is man and wife, man and wife is one flesh, and so . . . my **mother**! *(To his classmates)* Come, for England!

King: (Gesturing for the young men to go.) Follow him! I'll have him hence tonight! *(He watches them leave hurriedly, and then he speaks to himself.)* And, the present **death** of Hamlet—do it, England! *(He leaves with the weeping Queen.)*

(Servants remove the thrones and put up the sea-coast strip. Hamlet and his classmates enter, meeting a Norwegian army captain. They bow.)

Announcer 1: On the way to board the ship for England, Hamlet sees an army on the sea-coast.

Hamlet: (To the Captain) Good sir, whose powers are these?

Captain: They are of Norway, sir.

Hamlet: How purposed, sir?

Captain: Against Poland.

Hamlet: Who commands them, sir?

Captain: The nephew to old Norway, Fortinbras.

Hamlet: I humbly thank you, sir. *(The Captain bows and leaves. The Prince speaks to his classmates.)* I'll be with you straight. Go a little before. *(Rosencrantz and Guildenstern bow and leave reluctantly.)*

Announcer 2: Seeing the example of warlike Fortinbras, Hamlet regrets he has not revenged his father's murder.

Hamlet: (Feeling guilty) How all occasions do inform against me and spur my dull revenge! I do not

know why yet I live to say, "This thing's to do,"
sith I have cause and will and strength and
means to do it. *(Swearing an oath forcefully.)* O,
from this time forth, my thoughts be bloody, or be
nothing worth! *(He leaves, following his classmates.)*

*(The servants remove the sea-coast strip and put
the thrones in the alcove. The King and Queen enter with Horatio and others, much distressed.)*

Announcer 1: At court, there is a new tragedy. Because Hamlet killed her father, Ophelia has gone
mad.

*Ophelia: (Entering, her dress untidy and her hair un-
combed, she looks around.)* Where is the beaute-
ous Majesty of Denmark?

Queen: (Gently) How now, Ophelia?

Ophelia: (Bewildered) Nay, pray you, mark:
(Chanting) He is dead and gone, lady,
        He is dead and gone,
        At his head a grass-green turf,
        At his heels a stone.
(She kneels, pulls at her hair, and weeps.)

King: (In a kind voice) How do you, pretty lady?

Ophelia: (Rising and giggling) Well, God 'ild you!
They say the owl was a baker's daughter. *(Sur-
prised)* Lord, we know what we are, but know not
what we may be! *(Puzzled)* I hope all will be well.
My brother shall know of it! *(She curtseys to them
all as she leaves.)* Good night, ladies. Good night,
good night . . . . *(She runs away, laughing.)*

King: (To Horatio) Follow her close, I pray you. *(Horatio leaves.)* O this is the poison of deep grief. *(He embraces his weeping Queen.)* O Gertrude, Gertrude! First, her father slain. Next, your son gone. Last, her brother is in secret come from France . . . . *(Loud cries come from offstage.)*

Queen: (Alarmed) Alack, what noise is this?

Announcer 2: Ophelia's brother Laertes has returned from France. And the Danish people, protesting Polonius' murder, want to elect Laertes King.

Horatio: (Rushing in) Save yourself, my lord! The rabble cry, "Laertes shall be King! Laertes King!"

(With shouts and crashing noise, Laertes enters with armed men.)

Laertes: (Waving his sword angrily at King Claudius.) O thou vile King, where is my father?

King: (Sadly) Dead.

Laertes: Let come what comes, I'll be revenged most thoroughly for my father! *(He puts his sword point on the King's chest.)*

King: I am guiltless of your father's death!

Noble: (Standing aside at the door.) Let her come in!

Laertes: (As his pretty little sister enters with a basket of wildflowers, scattering them about.) O rose of May, dear maid, kind sister, sweet Ophelia . . . *(She looks at him blankly and turns away.)* O heavens, is it possible a young maid's wits should be as mortal as an old man's life?

Ophelia: (She gives the Queen the herb of sorrow.)
There's rue for you, and here's some for me. *(She speaks sharply, as if the Queen caused her own woe.)* O, you must wear your rue with a difference!

Ophelia: (Dancing quietly) You must sing, "Down, adown, and you call him adown-a." O how the wheel becomes it! It is the false steward that stole his master's daughter.

(She stops and gives out flowers to them, telling their meaning. To Laertes) There's rosemary. That's for remembrance. Pray you, love, remember! *(To Horatio)* And there is pansies. That's for thoughts. *(To the King)* There's fennel for you, and columbines. *(She gives the Queen the herb of sorrow.)* There's rue for you, and here's some for me. *(She speaks sharply, as if the Queen caused her own woe.)* O, you must wear your rue with a difference! *(To others)* There's a daisy. I would give you some violets, but they withered all when my father died. *(Grief-stricken)* They said he made a good end. God have mercy on his soul . . . and of all Christian souls, I pray. *(In farewell, happily)* God be with you! *(She runs off.)*

Laertes: (A cry of despair) O God!

King: Laertes, I pray you, go with me! *(He leads the young man off, talking to him silently as they go. The Queen and others follow, except for Horatio. A pirate enters with three letters.)*

Announcer 1: Now comes news of Hamlet's quick return.

Pirate: (Handing Horatio one of the letters.) There's a letter for you, sir. If your name be Horatio.

Horatio: (Opening the letter and reading.) "Horatio, ere we were two days old at sea, a pirate of very warlike appointment gave us chase! *(Horatio looks at the pirate, who grins and waves acknowledgment.)* In the grapple I boarded them. Let the King have the letters I have sent. These good fellows will bring thee where I am. Rosencrantz and Guildenstern hold their course for England. Farewell. Hamlet."

King: (Entering, his arm about Laertes.) I loved your father, and . . . *(To Horatio)* How now, what news?

Horatio: Letters, my lord, from Hamlet. *(He takes them from the pirate and gives them to the King.)* This to your Majesty, this to the Queen.

King: (Reading) "High and mighty, tomorrow I shall recount the occasion of my sudden and more strange return. Hamlet." And in a postscript here, he says, "Alone." *(He gestures to Horatio and the pirate, who bow and leave.)*

Laertes: Let him come! *(He draws his dagger.)*

King: Laertes, will you be ruled by me? I will work him to an exploit under the which he shall not choose but fall! Even his mother shall call it "accident." *(Laertes listens intently.)*

Announcer 2: Together the King and Laertes plan to kill Hamlet. The King suggests a fencing match, with Laertes using a sword without a safety button.

King: You have been talked of since your travel for art and exercise in your defence and for your rapier most especially. *(Laertes draws his sword and smiles.)* Sir, this report did Hamlet so envy that he could nothing do but wish and beg your coming to play with him. *(Laertes touches the sharp tip of his blade and practices a lunge.)* We'll bring you together and wager on your heads. With ease, you may choose a sword **un**-bated, and in a pass-of-practice requite him for your father!

Announcer 1: Laertes will not only use a sharp-pointed sword, but he will poison it as well.

Laertes: I will do it! *(He takes out a small vial of poison from his pocket.)* And for that purpose, I'll touch my point with this, that if I gall him slightly, it may be death!

Announcer 2: The King plans to poison him also.

King: Soft, let me see. I have it! When in your motion you are hot and dry, and that he calls for drink, I'll have prepared him a chalice . . . *(A loud cry sounds offstage.)* But stay, what noise? *(The Queen enters, crying. The King goes to steady her.)*

Queen: Your sister's . . . drowned, Laertes!

Laertes: (Stunned) Drowned! O where . . . .

Queen: (Pointing offstage) There is a willow grows aslant a brook that shows his hoar leaves in the glassy stream. There with fantastic garlands did she come of crow-flowers, nettles, daisies and long-purples.

Announcer 1: Ophelia tried to hang her flowers on the willow tree by the stream. A bough broke, and she fell into the brook. She floated for a while, singing, till the water pulled her down.

Queen: There on the pendent boughs her coronet weeds clambering to hang, an envious sliver broke, when down her weedy trophies and herself fell in the weeping brook. Her clothes spread wide. And, mermaid-like, awhile they bore her up, which time she chanted snatches of old tunes. But long it could not be, till that her garments, heavy with their drink, pulled the poor wretch from her melodious lay . . . to muddy death.

Laertes: (Overcome) Alas, then, she is drowned?

Queen: (Her voice shakes.) Drowned, drowned . . . .

Laertes: (Hiding his face in his hands.) Adieu, my lord. *(He leaves, shaking his head with grief.)*

King: Let's follow, Gertrude. Let's follow! *(They leave to comfort the young man.)*

ACT V

(The servants remove the thrones and place the grave-yard strip. Behind the strip, on his knees, the Sexton digs a grave and throws a legbone into the air.)

Announcer 1: Hamlet and Horatio meet in the grave-yard of Elsinore Castle. *(Quietly Hamlet enters with Horatio.)*

Sexton: (Chanting a song.)
    In youth, when I did love, did love,
        Methought it was very sweet,
    To contract, O, the time, for ah, my behove,
        O, methought there was nothing meet!
(He stops to drink from a leather bottle.)

Hamlet: (Curious) Whose grave's this, sirrah?

Sexton: Mine, sir. *(He grins and drinks again.)*

Hamlet: (Smiling) What man dost thou dig it for?

Sexton: For no **man**, sir! *(He chuckles.)*

Hamlet: What woman then?

Sexton: For none neither! *(He laughs at his own joke.)* One that **was** a woman, sir, but—rest her soul!— she's dead! *(He shows a skull.)* Here's a skull now hath lain you in the earth three-and-twenty years.

Hamlet: (Curiously) Whose was it?

Sexton: (Laughing) A mad rogue! This same skull, sir, was Yorick's skull, the King's jester!

Hamlet: Alas, poor Yorick! I knew him, Horatio.

Hamlet: Let me see! *(He picks it up thoughtfully.)*

Announcer 2: Yorick, the King's jester or clown, was Hamlet's childhood friend.

Hamlet: Alas, poor Yorick! I knew him, Horatio. A fellow of infinite jest, of most excellent fancy. He hath borne me on his back a thousand times. *(He speaks to the skull.)* Where be your songs, your flashes of merriment that were wont to set the table on a roar? *(He pretends to listen for an answer.)* Not one now? *(He looks offstage, putting down the skull.)* But soft—here comes the King, the Queen, the courtiers.

(He and Horatio go to one side, as the King, Queen, Laertes, a Priest, and others enter with the body of Ophelia on a stretcher, covered with a veil. The Sexton climbs out of the grave as the Priest makes the sign of the Cross and gestures for the men to put Ophelia into the grave.)

Laertes: (In tears, as the pallbearers lower Ophelia into the grave.) Lay her in the earth, and from her fair and unpolluted flesh may violets spring!

Hamlet: (Stunned) What, the fair Ophelia?

Queen: (Scattering flowers over the grave.) Sweets to the sweet. Farewell!

Laertes: (To the Sexton) Hold off the earth awhile, till I have caught her once more in mine arms! *(He leaps into the grave to hug his little sister one last time, bending over behind the ground strip.)*

Hamlet: (Coming forward) What is he whose grief

bears such an emphasis? This is I, Hamlet the Dane! *(He too leaps into the grave. He and Laertes wrestle.)*

Laertes: The Devil take thy soul! *(The courtiers rush to separate them and drag them out of the grave.)*

Hamlet: Why, I will fight with him! I loved Ophelia!

King: O, he is mad, Laertes!

Hamlet: (Sadly to Laertes) What is the reason that you use me thus? But no matter. The cat will mew and dog will have his day! *(He runs off, Horatio following him. The others exit slowly.)*

(The servants remove the graveyard strip and bring on the thrones as Hamlet and Horatio enter.)

Announcer 2: Hamlet tells how the King sent him to England, asking the English to kill him.

Announcer 1: But Hamlet stole the letter at night and wrote another one, asking that Rosencrantz and Guildenstern be killed.

Hamlet: Up from my cabin in the dark, to unseal their Grand Commission, I found, Horatio, an exact command: my head should be struck off!

Horatio: (Horrified) Is it possible?

Hamlet: (Nodding) I sat me down, devised a new Commission, that he should the "bearers" put to death. Now the next day was our sea-fight.

Horatio: So Guildenstern and Rosencrantz go to it. *(He makes the Sign of the Cross, as Hamlet nods bitterly. Horatio looks offstage.)* Peace, who comes here?

Announcer 2: A nobleman, Osric, comes to ask Hamlet to take part in the fencing match with Laertes.

Osric: (An over-dressed noble, he makes a fancy bow, waving his hat.) Sir, here is newly come to court Laertes. The King, sir, hath laid, sir, that in a dozen passes between yourself and him, he shall not exceed you three hits.

Hamlet: Sir, let the foils be brought, the gentleman willing. I will win for him an I can. *(Osric exits with another fancy bow.)*

Horatio: You will lose this wager, my lord.

Hamlet: I do not think so. Since he went into France, I have been in continual practice. I shall win.

Horatio: (Worried) Nay, good my lord . . . .

Announcer 1: But melancholy Hamlet thinks Fate decides even the death of a little bird. He is prepared to meet his end when it comes.

Hamlet: There's a special Providence in the fall of a sparrow! *(He thinks of his death.)* If it be now, tis not to come. If it be not to come, it will be now. If it be not now, yet it will come. The readiness is all!

(The King and Queen enter and sit on the thrones. Others follow. Laertes comes in with Osric, who carries the foils. The King makes the swordsmen shake hands.)

King: Come, Hamlet. Come and take this hand from me! *(He puts Laertes' hand into Hamlet's.)*

Hamlet: *(To Laertes)* Give me your pardon, sir. *(With sorrow.)* I've done you wrong. But pardon it as you are a gentleman.

Laertes: *(Pretending friendship)* I do receive your offered love like love and will not wrong it.

Hamlet: *(To Osric, who is judge.)* Give us the foils.

Laertes: Come, one for me! *(He chooses one without a safety button and, turning his back, quietly smears the sharp tip with poison.)*

Hamlet: *(Testing a sword)* This likes me well.

King: *(To servants who bring in wine, cups, and a table.)* Set me the stoops of wine upon that table.

Hamlet: *(As they take positions and salute each other with their swords.)* Come on, sir.

Laertes: Come, my lord!

(Osric gives the signal, and the two young men cross swords. Laertes slashes angrily. Hamlet parries the blows and scores a hit on Laertes.)

Hamlet: One!

Laertes: No!

Osric: *(As judge)* A hit, a very palpable hit! *(All applaud Hamlet, who bows to them.)*

King: Give me drink! *(He takes a wine-cup and holds up a ring.)* Hamlet, this pearl is thine. Here's to thy health. *(He drinks off half the wine and puts the poisoned ring into the cup, which he hands to Osric.)* Give him the cup!

Hamlet: (Waving Osric aside) I'll play this bout first. Set it by awhile. Come! *(Osric puts the cup on the table. The fight continues. Hamlet again lunges and steps back.)* Another hit!

Laertes: (Angrily) A touch, a touch, I do confess.

Queen: He's fat and scant of breath. *(She rises and gives Hamlet her handkerchief.)* Here, Hamlet, take my napkin. Rub thy brows. *(He wipes off the sweat, as the Queen takes up the wine-cup with the poison ring in it.)* The Queen carouses to thy fortune, Hamlet! *(She lifts the cup in a toast.)*

King: (Alarmed) Gertrude, do not drink!

Queen: I will, my lord. I pray you, pardon me. *(She drinks happily.)*

King: (Horrified, to Laertes) It is the poisoned cup!

Laertes: (To himself, shaking his head.) Tis almost 'gainst my conscience!

Hamlet: (Taking up his foil again.) Come, Laertes!

Laertes: Come on! *(They fight back and forth, stopping to catch their breath in separate corners.)*

Osric: Nothing, neither way!

Laertes: (To Hamlet, who is resting.) Have at you now! *(He stabs Hamlet's arm. Hamlet, startled, strikes the poisoned foil to the ground with his own weapon. Seeing the sharp tip, he puts his foot on it and gives his own sword to Laertes. Then he takes Laertes' poisoned sword.)*

Hamlet: (Grimly) Nay, come again! *(They fight, and Laertes is wounded with the poisoned tip. The Queen becomes faint, slumping to the floor.)*

Osric: Look to the Queen there, ho!

Horatio: They bleed on both sides! *(He and Osric separate the fighters.)*

Osric: (To Laertes) How is it, Laertes?

Laertes: (Looking at his poisoned wounds.) Why, Osric, I am justly killed with mine own treachery!

Hamlet: (Going to his mother) How does the Queen?

Queen: (With her last strength) The drink, the drink! O my dear Hamlet . . . the drink, the drink! I am poisoned! *(She dies.)*

Hamlet: (A great shout) Ho, let the door be locked! Treachery!

Laertes: (Weakly) Hamlet, thou art slain! In thee there is not half an hour of life. The instrument is in thy hand, envenomed. *(Hamlet and Horatio inspect the tip of the sword.)* Lo, here I lie, never to rise again. Thy mother's poisoned! *(He points.)* The King . . . the King's to blame!

Hamlet: The point envenomed too? *(The King rises to escape, but Hamlet stabs him with the poisoned sword.)* Then, venom, to thy work! *(He takes the*

Hamlet: The point envenomed too? *(The King rises to escape, but Hamlet stabs him with the poisoned sword.)* Then, venom, to thy work!

poisoned wine and pours it into the King's mouth.)
Here, thou murderous Dane, drink off this potion.
Follow my mother! *(The King drinks and dies.)*

Laertes: (Slowly falling to the floor.) Exchange forgive-
ness with me, noble Hamlet! *(As they clasp hands,
Laertes dies.)*

Hamlet: (To Laertes, as he feels the poison work.) I
follow thee. *(To his faithful friend)* Horatio, I am
dead. *(As Horatio helps Hamlet sink to the floor,
trumpets sound.)* What warlike noise is this?

Osric: (Looking offstage) Young Fortinbras, with con-
quest come from Poland.

Hamlet: O, I die, Horatio! *(He clasps hands with his
good friend, as his voice grows hoarse.)* But I do
prophesy the election lights on Fortinbras. He
has my dying voice. So tell him . . . the rest is
silence. *(He dies in Horatio's arms.)*

Horatio: (In a broken voice) Now cracks a noble heart!
(A last farewell) Good night, sweet Prince! And
flights of angels sing thee to thy rest! *(He closes
Hamlet's eyes and lays him gently down.)*

Announcer 2: The young Norwegian Prince Fortinbras, Hamlet's cousin, comes to witness the tragic
scene.

*Fortinbras: (A fine-looking warrior, he enters and
stops amazed at the royal dead. With him come his
nobles.)* O proud Death, that thou so many
princes at a shot so bloodily hast struck!

Horatio: (Rising, he addresses Fortinbras.) Give order that these bodies high on a stage be placed to the view. And let me speak to the world how these things came about. *(He picks up the King's crown and offers it to Prince Fortinbras.)*

Fortinbras: (Looking at the crown sadly.) For me, with sorrow I embrace my fortune. I have some rights of memory in this kingdom. *(As he puts on the crown, he turns to his officers.)* Let four captains bear Hamlet like a soldier to the stage! *(With deep respect)* For he was likely, had he been put on, to have proved most royally! Take up the bodies. *(He raises his arm in command.)* Go, bid the soldiers shoot!

(With reverence, four lords lift Hamlet high on their shoulders and carry him off slowly, with solemn music and the boom of drums and cannon.)

The End

(Editor's Note: We hope you have liked this short edition of the play. Now you can enjoy the stage productions and the original full-length script even more. As you continue to study Shakespeare, you will find that he can be a pleasure all your life!)